HELLO, DREAMER!
POEMS & DREAMS

ANITHA KRISHNAN

DREAM PEDLAR PUBLICATIONS

Copyright © 2021 by Anitha Krishnan

All rights reserved.

No part of this book may be reproduced in any form or by any electronic or mechanical means, including information storage and retrieval systems, without written permission from the author, except for the use of brief quotations in a book review.

Ebook ISBN: 978-1-7752278-5-4

Paperback ISBN: 978-1-7752278-2-3

Cover stock image 'Silhouette Fairy Against Moon' by upstudio on Depositphotos

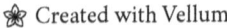 Created with Vellum

For The Dream Pedlar

*In these verses is all the love I didn't know
how to give you all those years ago*

Also for Dhruv & Abhinav

Love always

*Dreams for one,
dreams for all,
some dreams to last all day,
some for when the night falls.*

~ The Dream Pedlar

CONTENTS

Foreword	xi
1. Say Cheese!	1
2. Who am I?	2
3. Wild Spirit	3
4. Sonata	4
5. Night-time Tales	5
6. Message in a Bottle	6
7. Balancing Act	7
8. Optical Illusion	8
9. Lock and Key	9
10. Puzzle	10
11. Nostalgia	11
12. Responsibility of a Star	12
13. Occasional Lovers	13
14. Hidden	14
15. Time	15
16. In Remembrance	16
17. Noughts & Crosses	17
18. Marketplace	18
19. A Worn-Out Melody	19
20. A Magic-Maker Accused	20
21. The Magic-Maker's Rebuttal	21
22. Homage to Death	22
23. The Art of Storytelling	23
24. Kiss	24
25. Imprinted	25
26. Transformed by Love	26
27. When Words Fail	27
28. Bedtime Longings	28

29. Distorted — 29
30. A Definition — 30
31. Devotion — 31
32. Stuck — 32
33. A Love Song for You — 33
34. Treasures of You — 34
35. Love Notes — 35
36. War and Peace — 36
37. Prisoner's Dilemma — 37
38. Fan Following — 38
39. Relativity — 39
40. Good Job! — 40
41. Contradictions — 41
42. Twisting Time — 42
43. Making Way for Darkness — 43
44. Light in the Dark — 44
45. When the Kookaburra Sings — 45
46. Mind versus Heart — 46
47. Happy Birthday! — 47
48. Things that Escape — 48
49. Hiraeth — 49
50. Going Around in Circles — 50
51. A Traveller's Lament — 51
52. Heartbroken — 52
53. A Drunkard's Dance — 53
54. Reframing — 54
55. View Without a Window — 55
56. Niggling Sand — 56
57. Led Astray — 57
58. Counterpoises — 58
59. Pain — 59
60. Winter Chill — 60
61. Cure for Claustrophobia — 61
62. World of Imagination — 62
63. Borrowed Light — 63
64. Love, Defined by Absence — 64

65. Love Note to the Sun	65
66. Lending Meaning to a Quest	66
67. Fallen Words	67
68. Sources of Darkness and Light	68
69. Sound of Time	69
70. Seeking You	70
71. Existence in Full Bloom	72
72. Worship	74
73. Funeral for a Season	75
74. Fire and Smoke	76
75. Blinding Light	77
76. Soulmates	78
77. Only One Wish	80
78. Tales for the Spellbound	81
79. Loquacious Once More	82
80. Flight of Joy	84
81. Shape-Shifting Moon	86
82. Your Ephemeral Song	88
83. Weight of Absence	89
84. In Which I Reveal my Sources	90
85. Happiness, Intoxicated	91
86. Christmas!	92
87. Hide-and-Seek	93
88. No More Uncertainty	94
89. Mysteries in the Dark	95
90. Train Journeys	96
91. Tricks of the Moon	97
92. End of the Quest	98
93. From River to Ocean	99
94. A New Year	100
95. Without Rhyme or Reason	101
96. Enough Said	102
97. Tell Me About Yourself, O Beloved!	103

98. The Beginning of An Ending	105
99. Now What?	107
100. Last Words	108
Author's Note	111
Also by Anitha Krishnan	113
About the Author	115

FOREWORD

In the summer of 2015, I embarked on a 100 day project with a plan to write short poems.

Each day I typed a few lines and made them look beautiful using an amazing app called Notegraphy.

I shared these poems on social media. Loved ones encouraged me as I tried to maintain a daily streak and often missed but always came back and eventually completed the project.

The endeavour lasted 155 days, beginning in Montréal, Canada in July 2015, continuing in Toronto, and drawing to a close in Sydney, Australia that December.

FOREWORD

Looking back now, what I remember the most about this undertaking is the sheer delight I discovered in simply writing these verses and sharing them with family and friends.

On occasion, a friend would ask for a poem on a particular theme or mood. That's how *A Magic-Maker Accused*, *The Magic-Maker's Rebuttal*, and a few other poems came about. *A Traveller's Lament* struck a chord with many. *Responsibility of a Star* is one I hold dear because I clearly remember the joy I felt when the last line of the verse came to me after much deliberation and thought. I wrote *Happy Birthday!* to wish my husband on his birthday that year.

Plans for compiling and publishing these verses emerged only this summer (2021), more than six years since I set out on the adventure of writing them. Much has transpired in these years.

Our little one came into our lives, which led some readers to ask if *Without Rhyme or Reason* had been an announcement of his imminent arrival. (It hadn't.) Other books were written and published. We lived in many different places before coming to call Burlington, Ontario home. I fell in and out of love with writing—more precisely, the making-a-living-as-a-writer part of it—over and over again. And, of course, 2020 happened too!

So in many ways, returning to these long-ago verses brought back much of the delight and innocence that had suffused my writings all those years ago. It reminded me of how pleasurable writing could be when I simply put pen to paper and see what emerged. I hope you find the verses in this book just as enchanting.

~ Anitha
September 2021

SAY CHEESE!

DAY 1

*T*hunder roars like an angry lioness.

Lightning cracks like a rider's whip.

Look! A camera in the skies.

I bet the Gods have brought out their selfie sticks.

WHO AM I?

DAY 2

I am the dream you see
with eyes shut tight.
I am the dream that dies
when you wake to the morning light.

WILD SPIRIT

DAY 3

Yours is the song of the wilderness,

the ecstatic dance of the untethered,

so long as from doubt and fear

your spirit remains unfettered.

SONATA

DAY 4

Your voice warms my soul

like golden sunshine.

Your melody washes over me

like a psychedelic dream.

Your verses are etched on my heart,

deeper than the lines on my palm.

I hear you from afar

for it is your song I have become.

NIGHT-TIME TALES

DAY 5

*W*here the nights are sleepless

and the stars restless,

blinking in the Stygian skies,

there,

under the watchful gaze

of the shape-shifting moon,

is where the unfinished stories lie.

MESSAGE IN A BOTTLE

DAY 6

I etched my poetry on grains of sand

but the ocean lured all the words away.

Perhaps, like a message in a bottle,

my verses will wash up on your shores someday.

BALANCING ACT

DAY 7

We dance through space and time

as if on a tricksy tightrope walk,

imagination morphing into memory,

one step in the future,

another in the past.

OPTICAL ILLUSION

DAY 8

*L*ike orphaned shards of broken glass,

your heart lies in a million pieces and one,

but scoop them all into a kaleidoscope

and see how beautiful you grow at every turn.

LOCK AND KEY

DAY 9

You are a treasure chest sunk to the bottom of the ocean,

the burden of your loot too heavy to bear.

How much longer will you carry within

the only key to unlock yourself?

PUZZLE

DAY 10

The dots lie scattered farther than the eye can see.

Skip from one step to the next,

take baby steps, or leap over giant walls

for when you look back

you know you will clearly see

the mysterious line that connects them all.

NOSTALGIA

DAY 11

There is a hollow
at the base of my throat
that wells up at the memory of you,
where grief gathers, uninvited,
and unspoken words lose their way,
from where even the warmest scarves
fail to keep the winter chill away.

RESPONSIBILITY OF A STAR

DAY 12

Mine is not to be the lone star.

Mine is not to shine

the brightest of them all.

Mine,

like that of a million others,

is to play my part really well

in keeping the blackness

pinned to the skies above after nightfall.

OCCASIONAL LOVERS

DAY 13

No sheets of satin for her,
no scented candles,
no kisses in the moonlight.
Hers is the tale of hasty encounters,
of cheap thrills under neon lights,
of strange men who slip in
through the back door
and pretend to be her lover for a night.

HIDDEN

DAY 14

Thoughts are pressed

beneath the creases on your forehead.

Questions lurk voicelessly on your lips.

Secrets are tucked

into the folds of your skin.

I reach out to unravel you

only to lose myself

in the maze you hide within.

TIME

CHAPTER 15

Find precious moments of time

scattered throughout the day

like little beads of silver and gold.

Stitch them into a patchwork quilt for the night,

and weave your dreams for tomorrow into its folds.

IN REMEMBRANCE

DAY 16

*L*ying awake on a sleepless night,
I sift through my memories for some solace

and try to piece together in my mind

the hazy contours of your forgotten face,

and sometimes I remember

who you really were,

not merely who I wanted you to be.

NOUGHTS & CROSSES

DAY 17

*Y*ou cross.

I scribble a nought.

Cross, then a nought,

you cross, then drag a line.

Is the game over?

Or will you play again?

I like it when you win,

for what's yours is also mine.

MARKETPLACE

DAY 18

On grey cobblestoned streets,

    by the banks of endless rivers,

they peddle lover's breath and baby socks,

moonlight beams and foxes' whispers,

dreams of rainbow colours,

love in a bottle,

even hope

from the bottom of Pandora's box.

A WORN-OUT MELODY

DAY 19

You are the song I play
on repeat mode,

in an endless loop.

I have committed to memory

your every note and refrain.

Each lilt and beat of you is familiar to me

as the rhythm of my own breath.

My body sways to your tune, effortlessly.

So I hit *Play*.

Then *Rewind*.

Again and again.

A MAGIC-MAKER ACCUSED

DAY 20

*H*e makes up stories,

tells terribly tall tales.

He twists and bends words out of shape,

then strings them together.

He creates new worlds, alters reality,

tricks me with a clever sleight of hand.

I think he must be the most skilled magician

or just a very eloquent liar.

THE MAGIC-MAKER'S REBUTTAL

DAY 21

Mine is the world of make-believe,

of half-truths and illusions,

all smoke and mirrors,

of legerdemain and delusions.

There is magic, no doubt,

but that makes it not untrue

for your truths rise from what has been

and mine soar from the artist's dream.

HOMAGE TO DEATH

DAY 22

O Death! You must love me so much.

How patiently you wait, biding your time,

as I go about my wayward life, untethered!

How can such love ever go unrequited?

And so when the time comes,

I shall run into your arms,

bearing the gift of a life fearlessly lived.

THE ART OF STORYTELLING

DAY 23

*A*ll too often we remember

how the story ends,

but can barely recall

how it all began.

So we conjure up plots and twists

for it to all make sense

and by our own madness

we are unwittingly entertained.

KISS

DAY 24

I trace your mouth with my eager lips.

Our breaths mingle and dance skywards

like tiny slivers of our souls

drifting together in the misty air.

IMPRINTED

DAY 25

Like the butterfly that leaves behind

her delicate colours on my skin,

your love has freckled my soul

with indelible imprints,

and now my heart will pay heed

to no voice but yours.

TRANSFORMED BY LOVE

DAY 26

The more I learn to love,

the more I cease to exist.

All that remains

is an empty nothingness.

Like the hollow of a bamboo flute,

I wait for your lips to brush against mine

and compose the melody

I am meant to become.

WHEN WORDS FAIL

DAY 27

My heart is sinking,
weighed down by its own sorrow,

for all the words strung together

are burdened by their own meaning

and fail to promise hope for the morrow.

BEDTIME LONGINGS

DAY 28

When darkness settles on our paths like dust

and the owl's hoot pierces the sleepy skies,

my world glides to a gentle halt.

Nothing can stir me now

but the melody of your voice

humming my favourite lullabies.

DISTORTED

DAY 29

Now I see you with the fuzzy sight of the intoxicated.

An obscure view

through a rain-streaked window,

vague,

unclear,

like the explanations you left behind for me.

A DEFINITION

DAY 30

My poetry is all the words strung together

often with emotion

but sometimes with silent spaces in between

where the unspoken words reside.

DEVOTION

DAY 31

Like a planet orbiting the sun,
I spin round and round, all around you,

ecstatic like the whirling dervish,

so eager am I to fill you with joy.

I will grow wings and hover like an angel.

Your wish shall be my every command

for you are the only God I worship.

STUCK

DAY 32

*A*nd then there are days
when the words simply won't come your way,

no poetry to ease the pain,

no lyrics to lift your spirits high,

and all you can do is sink into the earth,

close your eyes,

and imagine you can fly.

A LOVE SONG FOR YOU

DAY 33

My depths are immersed in your blues.

My waters race to kiss you at the horizon.

When the seekers stand at my shores,

quiet and still in the face of our love,

they know not where the ocean ends

nor where the sky begins.

TREASURES OF YOU

DAY 34

I dove into the depths of your world

to reach the treasure bed of oysters,

and there I found your precious pearls,

the ones that shine so bright

they blot out the light of the sun.

LOVE NOTES

DAY 35

Some I have stashed away
in a shoebox in the attic.
Some others are tucked
between pages of my favourite books.
A few I have carelessly lost
along the way, I am sorry,
but the one I can never forget
is the first love note
you ever wrote to me.

WAR AND PEACE

DAY 36

Look how gently the sun slips behind the shadows of the night!

How daintily the moon glides forth

ostentatiously decked in stolen light!

And when dawn breaks, hers is a graceful retreat,

for even in their eternal war, there is peace.

PRISONER'S DILEMMA

DAY 37

My heart flings herself against the cage of my chest

and clamours for your attention.

I shush her, but to no avail.

She has long ceased to be mine.

Won't you look after what is rightfully yours?

Else, teach her how to be in two places at once.

FAN FOLLOWING

CHAPTER 38

I run from afar and race with dawn.

My pace is quickened by my greed

to soak up all your morning light.

But sitting by the shores are your devotees,

who have waited through a sleepless night

to be drenched in your golden sunshine,

and I know theirs is the greater need.

RELATIVITY

DAY 39

There is a reason the skies are vast,

the oceans boundless,

and the mountains proudly tall.

It is to make all our heartaches and worries

appear piteously small.

GOOD JOB!

DAY 40

A walk home past the beach in the dark,

the taste of the salty air on my tongue,

the music of the waves crashing upon the shores,

are all my rewards

for a long day of jobs well done.

CONTRADICTIONS

DAY 41

*J*ust as the endless silence
carries the longest echoes,
and the gravest secrets ride
on the backs of whispers,
so too the bearer of love is the heart
that is lighter than a tiny bird's feather.

TWISTING TIME

DAY 42

You may not love me tomorrow,

but you do today.

Is that not enough? You admonish me.

Then teach me how to lose myself

in the here and now,

so I may stretch this moment of your love

to last an eternity.

MAKING WAY FOR DARKNESS

DAY 43

Twilight sweeps over the dark shadows

that cease to linger in its wake.

The curtains fall on yet another day

as night takes over for darkness's sake.

LIGHT IN THE DARK

DAY 44

Another day is soaked up by the night,

darkness shields the shadows

lurking in my land.

But tiny dots of light speckle the regions beyond

like gleaming crystals hidden in the grainy sand.

WHEN THE KOOKABURRA SINGS

DAY 45

A faint mewl rises

from the earth below.

No cat can wail like that,

but I know of a bird that does.

Bluebirds peal in the distance,

too early for churchgoers.

And there is that hysterical laugh again.

Is it a madman, or a kookaburra?

Oh, I need a Shazam for the songs of nature!

MIND VERSUS HEART

DAY 46

Look not into my shallow mind.

A million thoughts crease its surface

and shatter every reflection of yours.

But come, peer into my heart.

It waits, still and clear,

like a silver-backed mirror.

Come, and look just how beautiful you are!

HAPPY BIRTHDAY!

DAY 47

Shadows flicker on your face

in restless anticipation.

Happiness floats above the warm candlelight.

Your eyelashes tremble,

clinging on to the wish that is taking shape.

Come now, blow out the candles.

The momentary plunge into the dark

will give your wishes a good place to start.

THINGS THAT ESCAPE

DAY 48

*L*ike crepuscular rays

that pierce the sleepy clouds,

or moonlight beams

that light up headstones in the dark,

like the sliver of light

that escapes closed doors,

there are dreams that lurk

in hidden alleyways and forgotten shadows.

Simply another of those things

that somehow fell through the cracks.

HIRAETH

DAY 49

Like a vagabond,
I have scoured this earth

looking for a place

that will cure my heart of its restlessness.

But now I fear such a place does not exist

except in the hidden recesses of my mind,

and I can do little else but write about it.

GOING AROUND IN CIRCLES

DAY 50

The journey ahead is only as long

as the paths we've left behind.

But now my boots are muddy, my limbs sore,

my breath is short and catches in my throat,

the sun blinds my eyes,

the woods close in upon me,

and I stumble on in an endless loop.

So forgive me if my words collapse in between lines

and float around like alphabets in your soup.

A TRAVELLER'S LAMENT

DAY 51

O little bird!
   Come sing to me your sweetest song!

A song of all the days gone by,

of dewdrop dreams and lovers' sighs.

For in all my travels around the world

I have left pieces of my heart behind

in places that I may never return to

and I need something to remember them by.

HEARTBROKEN

DAY 52

There was a time my soul would bleed

into the songs I wrote for you.

But now you are gone,

swifter than a memory fading into the past,

and it is hard to believe

my heart once knew how to love.

A DRUNKARD'S DANCE

DAY 53

Like the waves of the sea,
cresting from afar,
I rise and fall, again and again,
to the silent rhythm of my trance,
all for a momentary glimpse of you,
standing by the shore,
until I wash up at your feet,
buoyed by my inebriated dance.

REFRAMING

DAY 54

There are all these memories jostling for space in my little head.

More gather at the threshold, waiting to be let in,

reminders of every little thing once done and said.

And so I weed out the bad ones from the good,

clear more space for the happier thoughts.

Maybe this would make the past in my head

a lot happier than it truly was.

VIEW WITHOUT A WINDOW

DAY 55

This room of mine is bereft of windows.

So on the ceiling I have painted

my personal patch of sky,

azure in one corner, ebony in another,

a place for night stars and dainty fairies to fly

just as they do in the dreams I see

behind closed eyes.

So when I wake up in this windowless world,

I will look up and know my happiness wasn't a lie.

NIGGLING SAND

DAY 56

The grains of sand, they cling to my feet.

The waves wash them away.

And then I make my way across the shore, tiptoeing on the sand.

But the grains, oh so annoying, they cling to my feet once more.

So I hurry back home to run a warm bath, and lie down in it.

My feet clean, free of the pesky sand at last,

now I can reminisce about the golden beach and the ocean's roar.

LED ASTRAY

DAY 57

All the wise men told me
to shush my boisterous mind
and trust the tiny voice of my heart
to guide the way.
But look where that has got me,
to raw wounds and broken songs.
So blame me not should I wonder
if it were my heart or the wise men
that led me astray.

COUNTERPOISES

DAY 58

What good is a diamond without its rough?

Or a pretty star without its black night?

You cannot look the sun in the eye.

Without the cover of clouds,

he shines just too bright.

Is not the lotus adored

for the murky depths she springs from?

Or the rose made more beautiful by her thorns?

So too my darkness will be the fertile soil

from which my divinity is born.

PAIN

❄

DAY 59

Even the wind howls on occasion,

worrying the clouds and the treetops.

The ocean groans, in deep guttural sounds.

The sun fades, an old silver coin

pressed into the colourless sky.

But we mistake their anguish for fury

or is it a convenient lie we tell ourselves?

For we know only too well

anger subsides sooner or later

but grief only lingers on.

WINTER CHILL

DAY 60

*I*t must be that I spend far too long in winter

for the cold has my heart in its icy clutch,

pressing inside my chest

with its frozen gnarled fingers.

Now that the summer sun in here

you'd think my fears would melt away,

but even the slightest breeze

knows well how to make me shudder.

CURE FOR CLAUSTROPHOBIA

DAY 61

Sometimes even the seas and the skies

would press upon my chest

with all their weight.

The stars and the infinite galaxies,

their black boundaries,

would close in on me.

And when I yearned to run away

it seemed there was nowhere left to go.

But now I know the world is

only as large or small

as my little heart imagines it to be.

WORLD OF IMAGINATION

DAY 62

When I stand by the shores, all I see is the endless ocean.

So I return home and look out the window.

Brown tiles of the Jones's house

yield into a small patch of sky

that I have to crane my neck to see,

but there I also find rainbow swings,

elves at work, pixie dust, mermaid fins,

and all the beautiful things I see in my mind's eye.

BORROWED LIGHT

DAY 63

In this search for stillness,

I yearn to be like the sun, unwavering,

unmoved by the turmoil of the planets around him.

But in truth I am like the moon,

the restless shape-shifter, truth-obscurer,

protector of lovers and thieves and cowards.

How can I be like the sun

when even my light is not my own?

LOVE, DEFINED BY ABSENCE

DAY 64

All the times I had love
I never quite knew what it was.

Now that I have let it go in my carelessness,

I know what it is only through its loss.

Love has a way of finding us through time and space,

but this time would I remember to cherish it?

LOVE NOTE TO THE SUN

DAY 65

O rising sun,

how you set the ocean on fire!

Even the dull taupe sand at my feet

glitters unabashedly like gold,

and I wonder if I laid bare to you

all the precious secrets of my heart,

will you please make it shine a little more

as if stardust were sprinkled on my soul?

LENDING MEANING TO A QUEST

DAY 66

This is the thing about roads

and the quest for truth.

The roads have no beginning, no end.

It is me and my journeys that are bound

within the confines of space and time.

Like the roads, the truth is

there is no truth,

and my quest exists only

to give my life some placatory meaning.

FALLEN WORDS

DAY 67

Our words fall like the last of the autumn leaves

and are quickly buried in the snow.

Winter is always so long

by the time spring comes around

the fallen words are forgotten,

the untold stories have changed,

and so have you,

and so have I.

SOURCES OF DARKNESS AND LIGHT

DAY 68

*H*ow easily does darkness exist

in the realms of outer space,

in the depths of the ocean,

buried under the aches of a troubled heart!

But the light, when it comes,

is always from a source

that burns unto itself,

then falls apart like a shooting star.

SOUND OF TIME

DAY 69

The mist rolls in from the seas,

bearing secrets from distant lands.

The waters help them carry their burden,

drowning whispers in the ocean's roar,

mysteries strewn in the glistening sand.

Hush, now!

Put a seashell to your ear and listen

to the sound of time passing you by.

SEEKING YOU

DAY 70

I look for you in the skies.

Which one of these twinkling stars are you?

I look for you in the woods.

Tell me,

which one of those exotic wildflowers are you?

My bewilderment amuses you.

Why only one of those? you ask.

Come find me in all of this world.

Imagine me in any shape, in any form, you propose.

. . .

O my beloved,

but grant me not such trespasses

for my imagination can do

no justice to your beauty!

EXISTENCE IN FULL BLOOM

DAY 71

*I*n your unconditional love I bloom,

a rose just made aware of her beauty.

Now that is all I know,

to blossom so fervently you can smell

the scent of my heart from afar.

But should I wilt before you return,

preserve me not

between the sheaves of your poetry.

. . .

Crush my remains instead,

so I can sublime away in the air around you

and wrap your being in my tender fragrance.

WORSHIP

DAY 72

I run to your altar, my heart set aflame

by a thousand desires burning in me for fulfilment.

All it takes is one look at your beatific face

for me to shed my longings

like drops of water gliding down a lotus leaf.

And I wonder what need I ever had

for anything other than to nestle

in your reassuring grace!

FUNERAL FOR A SEASON

DAY 73

*N*ow that the last of the autumn leaves have fallen,

the sky is shattered by grief.

It crumbles into flakes of frozen tears

that fall swiftly to the ground,

all its million pieces,

to lay its friends to rest

under a white blanket,

a warm grave to last all winter.

FIRE AND SMOKE

DAY 74

*L*ike smoke and fire,
never one without the other,
we prance together in a playful dance.
When your proud flames leap skywards
I come into being only in your presence.
And when you perish
in the dying embers of a festive bonfire,
I too gladly cease to exist.

BLINDING LIGHT

DAY 75

There were parts of me I wanted to hide

but even the bluest oceans were not

deep enough for me to bury my secrets.

And then you came along,

resplendent, bearing a light of your own,

and you shone so brightly on me

the world has now become blind

to all my imperfections.

SOULMATES

DAY 76

*H*ow strange it is
that I pine for you so much

when we haven't even met!

But I know how beautiful your face is,

how your music reverberates through my breath.

Could it be you were once

an inseparable part of me,

cleaved from my soul

when I turned my attention away from you?

. . .

And now all that remains of you in me

is all this inexplicable love

gushing from this fractured heart?

ONLY ONE WISH

DAY 77

*I*f there is only wish
you will grant me,
then make me so small
there will be room only for you
in my world, now so tiny,
and no other desire
shall dare slip past you
to seek refuge in me.

TALES FOR THE SPELLBOUND

DAY 78

*A*nd should I ever run out
of things to say to you,
remind me not to fade away
behind a veil of silence,
but to make things up and tell tall tales,
to spin stories from flax-golden yarn,
to peddle a few dreams
for you to remember me by
long after my sojourn in this world
has come to an end.

LOQUACIOUS ONCE MORE

DAY 79

Oh, there was so much I wanted to tell you

I penned these songs by moonlight.

Fussed over each verse, each melody,

for every little thing had to be perfectly right.

But the first sight of you renders me speechless.

All my songs quickly desert me.

Traitors!

How unworthy of you they proved!

I am ashamed.

So now in this eternal span of silence,

the only music I have

is the tuneless pulse of my guileless heart

who still wants to sing only for your attention.

FLIGHT OF JOY

DAY 80

The very thought of you
makes me soar.

I transcend

the invisible boundaries of this world.

Nothing can weigh me down now.

Light as a feather I drift

wherever the breeze blows me.

Everybody thinks I am a vagabond,

aimlessly lost in some psychedelic haze.

. . .

But only I know

you have instructed the wind

to gently guide me to your abode

and bring me to rest

in your soothing embrace.

SHAPE-SHIFTING MOON

DAY 81

Night after night,
the restless waters

break up the face of the moon

into a jillion smithereens of silver.

They steal her fragments

and tuck them into oysters

in a place where darkness gobbles up the light.

One night the moon fades away,

leaving no trace,

and the sea regrets his folly.

. . .

HELLO, DREAMER!

He lures her back

a few slivers at a time,

and we helplessly watch the moon

shape-shift until eternity.

YOUR EPHEMERAL SONG

DAY 82

Your voice is composed of all the obscure notes

that no instrument can play,

sweeter than the cry of the Indian koel

calling for her lover in the heat of May.

Your song rides unexpectedly on angel wings,

the melody gone before I can discern it,

and only my eager heart grasps and treasures

all the bewitching verses you sing.

WEIGHT OF ABSENCE

DAY 83

*A*n empty space sits heavy on my chest.

Sound knows not how to traverse this barrenness.

So the unspoken words remain pressed within my heart.

Their clamour is so loud

I can no longer hear you calling out my name.

IN WHICH I REVEAL MY SOURCES

DAY 84

Occasionally the wind drops,

the trees stand still, nearly lifeless,

even the birds know not to shatter the silence,

the waves settle, the ocean is a creaseless sheet of blue,

for their spirits have momentarily trooped away

into hidden shadows and secret tree hollows

where they write the poems

I will soon sing for you.

HAPPINESS, INTOXICATED

DAY 85

*H*appiness comes riding on the breeze,

settles gently on the windowsill,

soft to the touch, a delicate feather.

I ought to know better

than to reach out and grab her.

She will not be made to stay for long.

It is up to me to fall into step

and learn her inebriated dance.

CHRISTMAS!

DAY 86

The tree is up,

holding all the frosted glass baubles,

filled with oversized hopes and desires.

Drape her in bright tinsel and fairy lights

so when the stars peep in

through your window tonight

they will learn of all the secret things

you have wished for this year.

HIDE-AND-SEEK

DAY 87

In this game we play,

in which you hide and I seek

as if I am looking for a star in the night sky,

I see you everywhere I go.

And I think you are so clever

surely you won't be found so easily, not even in jest.

Or is that just a notion my mind has made up

so it can take some pride in this delightful quest?

NO MORE UNCERTAINTY

DAY 88

What would I ever do without you? I cry.

Why would you ever be without me? comes your reply.

MYSTERIES IN THE DARK

DAY 89

When darkness closes in upon you

and you stumble over your own shadow,

when doubt and fear become your plight,

I will stand there as a guiding light

or lurk behind you

as a strange creature of the night.

TRAIN JOURNEYS

DAY 90

Like rusty tracks we run forever
alongside each other,

like arm's-length lovers,

alone even when we are together.

TRICKS OF THE MOON

DAY 91

All the strange things happen in the forbidden darkness of the night

because no one wants to believe

what the moon conceals

in the shadows cast by her pilfered light.

END OF THE QUEST

DAY 92

Now that I have found you, what need have I for vapid words?

I am one with the roses in your garden.

How can I speak of their beauty with sincerity?

My heart throbs in the tender chest of the nightingale.

How can I be the one to sing of her dulcet tunes?

But am I not then ungrateful to shun the very path

that has led me all the way to your door?

FROM RIVER TO OCEAN

DAY 93

You are the vast, endless ocean,

and I am restless as the stream,

weary of its frenzied journey from the mountaintop.

I tumble towards you in haste,

anxious to empty myself into your being.

Now that I know how limitless your existence is,

I will no longer be confined to my petty boundaries.

A NEW YEAR

DAY 94

I remember this day.

It came last year too,

and all the years before.

Each time it unfolds

in a comically identical way.

Fireworks and promises, the whole shebang.

The only difference is made

by all the moments in between

that slip by

without warning

or recognition.

WITHOUT RHYME OR REASON

DAY 95

I have been awfully good this year.

Look at all the poetry I wrote!

With little regard for rhyme and reason, I admit.

Surely you will not hold that against me now, will you?

That is a concession you must allow me

for can there not be madness

when all year I have been carrying

two thumping hearts

within this frail being of mine?

ENOUGH SAID

DAY 96

So much have I written and said

now I am drowning in the din

of my own verses,

and my heart, like a raging volcano,

wants to spew more poetry.

So I simply reach in and rip her out.

There!

Now I can hear nothing but your silence

and I have never felt more alive.

TELL ME ABOUT YOURSELF, O BELOVED!

DAY 97

I look at you and wonder.

Were you naughty when you were younger?

Did you look up at the clouds

and see elephants and dinosaurs?

Did you lie awake at night and trace

the constellations with your fingers?

Did you cry when you hurt

or were you taught to hold back your tears?

. . .

Every little detail I want to learn about you

but one lifetime is not enough to hold all the answers.

THE BEGINNING OF AN ENDING

DAY 98

I see you in the vast blue yonder.

My journey has now almost come to an end.

I should be ecstatic I have found you at last,

my reward for these endless meanderings.

Then why am I sad?

A deep sense of loss engulfs me,

for everything familiar I am leaving behind.

Now I am afraid to find out what I really loved more?

You?

Or my illusory longing?

NOW WHAT?

DAY 99

*A*nd this is how, slowly, gently, the last jagged piece of my heart falls away.

Your light now shines through me

as if it were my own,

revealing you in all your indescribable glory.

Oh, so much fun it was to seek you

here and there and everywhere!

Now go, hide again.

Let me not deny other seekers

the pleasure that is rightfully theirs.

LAST WORDS

DAY 100

We will meet again
at the witching hour.
I will travel through the stars in my sky
till I reach the ones you see in yours.

Hopping over
those twinkling diamonds of light,
I will flit into your dreams
while you gently sleep tonight
and sprinkle stardust into your being.

. . .

HELLO, DREAMER!

So when you wake up to a dawn,

fresh and new,

you will know to view the world

through the delightful madness

now growing within you.

AUTHOR'S NOTE

Hello, Dreamer!

Thank you for reading this book!

If you enjoyed it, I hope you will consider writing a review—even a simple line or two—on your favourite book site.

Publishing is still driven by word of mouth, and when you leave a review it helps other readers decide this is a book worth reading.

I'm working hard on my forthcoming books, and knowing that readers might be interested in more of my works will certainly be very encouraging.

Thank you!

ALSO BY ANITHA KRISHNAN

In Search of Leo

A speculative fiction story on the vast range
of emotions that grief and loss can stir.

Dying Wishes

A new-adult contemporary fantasy novel set
in Burlington, Ontario and weaving Hindu
mythology and South Indian folklore into a
quest for belonging across different worlds –
the World of Mortals and the World of
Gods, India and Canada, the past and the
present, the world outside and the one
within.

ABOUT THE AUTHOR

Anitha Krishnan is a speculative fiction author and an award-winning poet. She lives in Burlington, Ontario with her husband and their cherished child.

Find more books and her blog on the writing life at thedreampedlar.com.

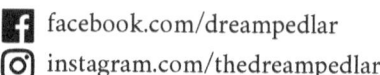 facebook.com/dreampedlar
instagram.com/thedreampedlar

www.ingramcontent.com/pod-product-compliance
Lightning Source LLC
Chambersburg PA
CBHW030911080526
44589CB00010B/247